FINDING PIECES OF ME IN LIFE, LOVE, PRAISE AND POETRY

May 12, 2021

Dear Rodney,

Thank you for your support. Hope you'll enjoy my poems. Take care & God bless you always.

Love,
Salva ♥

FINDING PIECES OF ME IN LIFE, LOVE, PRAISE AND POETRY

ROSELLE

Copyright © 2020 Roselle

All rights reserved.

ISBN 13: 9798683123895

For My Beloved Family

TABLE OF CONTENTS

Acknowledgments · xi

Self-Made Poet · 1
Field of Dreams · 3
Conquistador · 5
Cocoon · 7
They Danced · 11
The Wind Sings to Me · 13
Seafarer · 15
Forbidden Fruit · 17
Little Brother · 19
Mustard Seed · 21
Modern-Day Cinderella · 23
Planting Friendship · 25
I Can't Imagine · 27
Bind by IV Tubing · 29
Addicted to Love · 31
Starry, Starry Night · 35

Grave Cross Stick	37
Sailing	41
Backpacks	43
From Your Rib Cage	45
My Blue Sky	49
Burned Candle	51
Bridge	53
River	55
Little Brown Sparrow	57
Soft Wind	61
Stranger Danger	63
My Shell	67
Snowflake	69
Light Walks Into My Life	73
My Soul	77
Looking Glass	79
Graceful Shore	81
How Can I Thank You?	83
Counting	85
How I Read You	87
I Thank God for Poetry	89
True Happiness	91
The Deafening Silence	93
Chaos	95
Frontline	97
Hope for Humanity	99
My Pep Talk	101
With My Eyelids Closed	103

Into the Woods · 107
Before I Go to Sleep ·111
My Painting ·113

ACKNOWLEDGMENTS

2019 was a difficult year. After my daughter and I survived a major car accident, I was diagnosed with breast cancer. I felt the need to run to safety—which I found in poetry. It relieved me of my stress and freed my imagination, which yearned for peace in this chaotic world. Through my writing, I was able to express my deepest thoughts in ways I could not convey otherwise. A window of opportunity opened. I was able to embrace self-expression while also connecting with others who found comfort and familiarity in my words. I never thought life would lead me to publishing a book, especially one filled with poems. The obstacles I faced brought a deeper appreciation of life and a closer relationship with God, and I hope to share with the world my journey and passions through this collection of poems.

I am incredibly grateful to my family, especially to my three children, Faith, Hawke, and Lancelott. You are my strength and my inspiration.

To my two best friends, Sonia and Myrlande, who share my love of poetry: thank you for believing in me.

Self-Made Poet

SELF-MADE POET

Every word, every line, every stanza, or punctuation mark I left behind
Every joy, every pain
Every victory or shame
Every right and every wrong
Unerasable actions that made me strong
My memories I have written
And tucked in every poem
My life made me a poet
Who's hiding between the lines
If you have read them,
You'll know what's in my heart and in my mind.

Field of Dreams

FIELD OF DREAMS

At the crack of dawn
We rise to sow
To do the task
That we're assigned to do
A bountiful field of dreams
In this beautiful world we live in
We're all working together
In such a graceful scheme
He plowed the soil
I planted the seed
You built the drain to direct the water flow
While she provided some fertilizers
To help the plants grow
Each of us will be rewarded
With what we are all due
There is no difference
Between what you and I really do
In this bountiful field of dreams
In our hearts we all should know
That what really matters is
God makes all the plants grow.

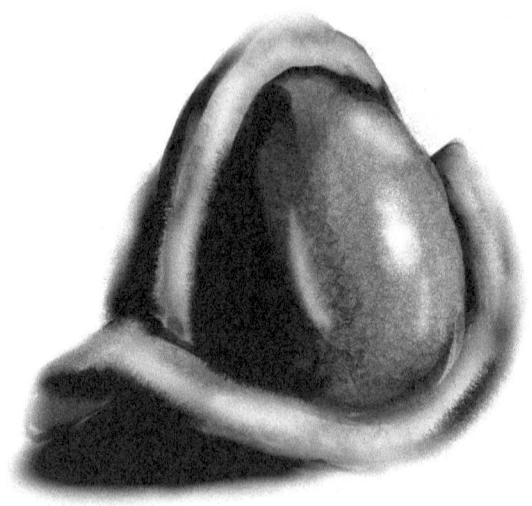

Conquistador

CONQUISTADOR

Wearing his cold metal armor
His tantalizing eyes with blinding luster
His powerful words that can surely capture
His touch that can make me weak
Before I knew it, I was kneeling down at his feet
Conquistador
He bound my arms with promises
He caged my heart with excuses
He lured me with his beguiling smile
He nourished me with attention for a little while
He has forgotten that I also had emotions
He left me and continued with his explorations
Conquistador
He made my eyes weep
He made my pen bleed
He made me build walls against his offense
But the irony of my defense
I vandalized the walls for his glory in excellence
And my defeat is in repeat
To my Conquistador of deceit

Cocoon

COCOON

I grew up in a city, where I could hear everything on the streets
From the engines of vehicles that are speeding
The children's voices on the streets while they're playing
The loud calling of the vendors to promote the products they're selling
Even the neighbor's voice when they're talking
The bakery is just across the street
They make the best pan desal, it's soft and sweet
I usually dip it in coffee before I eat
But the Taho in the morning is my favorite treat
Public transportation is very accessible and in variety
I like the fact that the commute is so easy
There's taxicab, tricycle, and the world-famous Jeepney
The only problem is the traffic, so you need to leave early
The streets are narrow and long
Some houses are made of cement and the others are called Barong-barong
You can hear someone belting out their favorite song
On their karaoke, which has been playing all night long
During Fiesta, there is always a street party in the neighborhood
Houses are open to everyone, serving different drinks and food
Most men are on their best behavior like they should
But some get too drunk, riots start, and the party gets screwed

In the place where I grew up, there is poverty
It taught me perseverance and humility
Places we live and the people we see
Some leave a mark on our personality
But it doesn't mean that we are their summary
Because I am my own identity
You and I, we're like butterflies
Our cocoon is not the best way to judge us if we can fly
So let's spread our wings, and we shouldn't be shy
Let our wings' beautiful colors magnify.

They Danced

THEY DANCED

I remembered my parents' love story
How my dad met my mom at a town party
They say she was a graceful dancer
And he was a lady charmer
My dad actually looked like Charles Bronson
They said my mom had a pretty face but common
She and her sister were the best dancers in town
The party was not complete if they're not around
He fell in love with her dance moves
Ballroom dancing was their kind of groove
I don't know how many times they danced
But the dance floor was where they started their romance
I never got the chance to see them do the Cha-Cha or Tango
All I saw was their dance that's slow
They would dance in the middle of our house
They showed us love and loyalty to their vows
On top of the palm leaf mat
Where my siblings and I gathered around to watch
They danced to the song of Andy Williams's "Moon River"
A sweet memory that I will always remember.

The Wind Sings to Me

THE WIND SINGS TO ME

The wind sings life
As soon as I heard your first cry
My sacrifices were all worthwhile
My child, your "wah" made me smile
The wind sings terror
Rumbles, whirs, and roars
Tornado came with so much power
Disaster is such a devastating encounter
The wind sings joy
Blowing the flame of the birthday candle
A grateful heart making a wish
Surrounded by the company she enjoys
The wind sings acclamation
Loud clapping and a standing ovation
Bright future for the new generation
Is celebrated during graduation
The wind sings love
Church bells ringing as the choir sings
A beautiful bride walking down the aisle
Toward the love of her life
The wind sings sorrow
Crying, sobbing, moaning, and howling
Wind carries the scent of floral wreath
Unable to dry the tears of the ones who weep.

Seafarer

SEAFARER

Their music is the sound of the waves and the birds that are flying by
The scent of the salty breeze is a constant aroma
Their visitors are the playful dolphins and so are the orcas
Trapped in the middle of the sea
Where the raging waves are not the adversary
But they fight with the sad emotion
That can lead to suicide or melancholic depression
Months or years of missing their loved ones
Working on the cargo ship is their main source of income
They're counting down from months to weeks, to days, and down to hours
That is the lonely life of all the Seafarers
My dad worked for so many years in the said trade
My few sweet memories of him will never ever fade
The shipping company he worked for claimed that it was a suicide
I was only six years old when my father died
So love your dad, your pop, or your father
Hug him tight, kiss his cheeks, and make him prouder
He worked so hard to put food on your table
Do not let him reach for that execution cable.

Forbidden Fruit

FORBIDDEN FRUIT

In the garden of lust
Lured by your beguiling chat
Rattling tales of pride
Oblivious of your lies
Teasing with hissing
Enticing the weak
Breaking all boundaries
Until their defeat
A taste of the forbidden
Entwined souls to sin
Jealousy of the fallen
Causing mankind's descent
All God's gifts were forsaken
By the ungrateful and rotten
Would I still be in existence
If the fruit of good and evil had not been eaten?

Little Brother

LITTLE BROTHER

I can't forget how you loved to belt out Yoyoy Villame's songs,
Especially your favorite "Si Filemon"
You sounded so funny, but I think that was your intention
You made me listen to your singing all day long
Having me back home, for you was a big celebration
I can still hear your high-pitched voice in my mind
To me, you were always sweet and always kind
When I passed the boards, you spread the news to our neighbors
Faster than the speed of light, you were the proudest little broadcaster
It's sweet knowing that you'll pick my dad over yours, if given a choice
Just having you as a little brother makes my heart rejoice
When others address you as half, I am always annoyed
They are the kind of people I always try to avoid
Your situation made you tough and brave
You learned to hide your feelings, especially your pain
The bike accident that led you to your grave
What if you had told our mom? In my head, that question still remains
Today is your birthday, my little brother
I know you're in heaven singing with all the angels
Beautiful moments with you, I will always remember
The nineteen years on this earth where you have blown your candles.

Mustard Seed

MUSTARD SEED

Tiny as can be
But just like you
God made me too
Planted in his garden
With his love to hearten
By moist soil that nurtures
Until I grow to mature
Little sunshine that's so warm
Just like his loving arms
Little rain that he sprinkles
To straighten my crinkle
Look how he nourished me
I sprouted so fast to see
This beautiful world he created
I am definitely fascinated
Look how tall I grew
No one expected and knew
That this mustard seed they denigrate
Has this much faith to generate.

Modern-Day Cinderella

MODERN-DAY CINDERELLA

Alas! It's midnight
It's too late, but you have to fight
You're running out of time
Others heard it but ignored the chime
Cinderella, run, run, run
Run as fast as you can
Your stepmother is in charge
She only cares about the institution at large
So like a hamster on a running wheel
You're trying to get your fill
You ran away from destitution
Now you're working like a dog in an institution
You left your glass slippers in a dream palace
It's the only place where you can join the upper class
You're running barely dressed and barefooted
Exposed to hazards yet you're supposed to be protected
There's no fairy godmother to save you
Only the fair people that you meet and there are few
Your Prince Charming was dressed decently
But he treated you with indecency
Cinderella, run, run, run
To your dreams as fast as you can
Let your mind be your carriage
To the dreamland where no one is savage.

Planting Friendship

PLANTING FRIENDSHIP

Friendship is a blessing
Blessing in a glass
Glass that can be broken, or it can make it last
The last thing we want is to break the trust
Trust that's important
Important for it to grow
Grow for all seasons
Seasons that often change
Change it shall weather
Weather-beaten or joyful all the time
Time shall find it true
True friendship that will survive
Surviving in this world with true friendship
Is a friendship for life
Thank you for being a friend.

I Can't Imagine

I CAN'T IMAGINE

I can't imagine how you feel
Hearing explosions almost everywhere
I can't imagine how you feel
After the trauma and in constant fear
I can't imagine how you feel
When it's cold or raining but there's no shelter
I can't imagine how you feel
When your stomach hurts because of hunger
I can't imagine how you feel
Counting the days when your end draws near
I can't imagine how you feel
When you can't breathe and gasp for air
I can't imagine how you feel
When you're locked in a cell with conscience clear
I can't imagine how you feel
Left all alone like no one cares
Forgive my ignorance for I am also in despair
But despite life's circumstances that's cruel and unfair
I can only imagine that God listens to all our prayers.

Bound by IV Tubing

BIND BY IV TUBING

Broken spirit, broken dreams,
broken promises, and broken hearts
Painted like a mosaic
And seen through the eyes that lost their spark
My hands are tied and my feelings concealed
Silent tears were shed, for your fate has been sealed
You have been through a lot
That knife made more than just a cut
What you lost is more than just a piece of flesh
You patched it up with faith, hope, and courage in a mesh
You're here for the promised cure to run through your veins
Hoping to kill the cancer that's causing you pain
Crippling desperation is worse than the side effects
Please continue fighting until your last breath
Let me pay you my respect as I perform my duty
I will sail in your ship while you cruise your memory
Tell me your stories and adventures
Show me those photographs that you captured
I would like to play your favorite song
While you and I sing along
Let me know you more than your health records
Your IV tubing binds us like an umbilical cord
I know nobody wants to be sick and become dependent
A hospital is the last place you want your time spent
So as you rest on that bed while your medication is dripping
My love and prayers for you are constantly pouring.

Addicted to Love

ADDICTED TO LOVE

I have a confession to make
Please read with an open heart and I hope you won't judge
It takes a long time to build a reputation but so easy to get it to smudge
My poetry is the proof of this eccentric fact
My emotions mixed up in words forming an abstract
I am an addict
I am so addicted to love
It's so hard to control yet so easy to have
From the moment I open my eyes
I am so grateful and high
Another day, another gift of love
He started it all, our Father from up above
I can feel love around me
I can hear love around me
I can smell love around me
I can see love around me
I can't contain my emotions
His gift of love for my salvation
He gave the greatest gift someone can ever give
Sometimes the truth I still can't perceive
I do feel ecstatic when I feel his magic
Even in the image of something that is tragic
Miracles of his love manifest

How my patients survive is an attest
I am so addicted to love
I can see it in your eyes
You have it too, please say no lies
Our world gets shaken when it's absent
Irrational behavior such as greed and vices will be present
I can hear love syncing
Birds singing, dolphins whistling, dogs barking
Even in humans cursing when they are talking
Every word from a loving heart
Spills a drop of love in a linguistic art
The scent of the flowers or the salty sea breeze
The aroma of the spices or from the lemon squeezed
The food served with love doesn't need to come from France
I can smell love in the kitchen even from a distance
Every tender touch this so-called love awakens
From a mother's hug, to a stranger's handshake, and flying kisses given
From a penny dropped to a beggar's tin can
To walking someone across the street while holding their hand
Your teacher's compassion to inculcate a lesson
Firefighters' courage after someone's arson
I can see the love in a caregiver's eyes
Who's trying to help their dying patient survive
Even with their foggy face shield and worn N95
I can go on and on with my love addiction
I have been studying the Bible for some instructions
Don't be scared even though it's contagious

Loving life is nothing serious
I am addicted to love, can't you see?
I love you all and hope you'll love me.

Starry, Starry Night

STARRY, STARRY NIGHT

On a starry, starry night
My heart sings Vincent's song of lamentation
No one can hear its harmony
As it echoes in my memory
On a starry, starry night
I questioned my deepest intentions
Will my tears reflect what I envisioned
As the moon and the stars are in their rightful position?
On a starry, starry night
Where a hundred thousand million stars are shining
My world shall sleep in peace
Knowing God's infinite grace.

Grave Cross Stick

GRAVE CROSS STICK

It's almost been a year since you passed
The grief of your loss seems to last
Sister, sister, I miss you so much
How can I forget your healing touch?
I am so sorry for being so unruly
I was so jealous of you because you're so pretty
I know I made you cry when you were in high school
I was too lazy to get up, and I was acting like a fool
When I forgot my school bag, you ran after that Jeepney
While I was just watching you with my eyes still sleepy
You never scolded me for that
You were so worried about this little brat
Sister, sister, I am sick
I miss your massages and how you would be there so quick
I still remember how you would crush that fresh ginger
And wipe it so gently with your tired loving fingers
Mother was not perfect and had some slack
But you were always there for me and filled that crack
You were my Athena for wisdom and courage
An Atlas in silence with all your carriage
I knew you were struggling
But you always kept everything in hiding
You always said you're okay
Even if your facial expression showed dismay

How can I forget that delicious Taho you bought?
How can I forget that medicine you brought?
How can I forget the memories we shared?
How can I forget the way you always cared?
Sister, sister, I am sick
I have a deep wound from your grave cross stick
I never had a chance to make up to you
It was too soon for you to say adieu.

Sailing

SAILING

I am sailing
In this ocean called life
Vast and relentless
I am in constant strife
I have nothing prepared
For this long journey
Just a life jacket of faith,
Oars full of courage, and a flare of hope
As I row the boat
Toward my destination
A couple of storms have passed
I never thought I could last
I did get tired, weary, and weak
I had thoughts of giving up so quick
But a bite from the bread of life
And a gulp of living water
Made me feel all right
So I continued to row the boat
In this ocean called Life
Hoping to reach my destination
As I paddle with all my might.

Backpacks

BACKPACKS

Backpacks, snacks, and bottled water
At the back of the minivan prepared for my travelers
Everyone was excited and ready for the mini adventure
Cross-country trip to enjoy the nature
The sky was blue and the sun was brightly shining
The white puffy clouds like cotton candy were slowly floating
From East Coast to West Coast was our itinerary
Hoping to reach our destination slowly but surely
We passed several states and visited some landmarks
My favorite was the landscape of Grand Canyon National Park
Standing on the side of the canyon's rim, I was speechless
Looking at the panoramic view, an experience that's priceless
Hues of red, orange, green, gray pink, brown, and violet rocks
How they're formed by the river currents is a known fact
It reminds me that life's challenges are like currents of a river
Aimed to shape our lives and make us better
Different states have beautiful sites worth visiting
Nature is full of wonders and worth exploring
It was summer of 2014, when we crossed the country
The view and the bonding is one of my fondest memories.

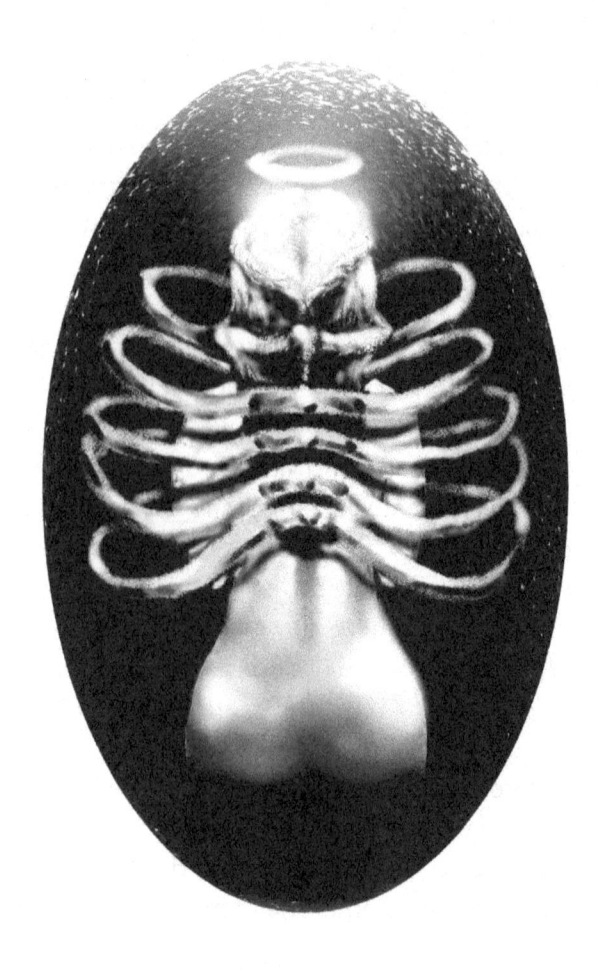

From Your Rib Cage

FROM YOUR RIB CAGE

Did you see me as the Peasant Girl of Vincent Van Gogh
Or as a seductive Egyptian Queen of Frank Frazetta
Or maybe the highest priced Leonardo Da Vinci's Mona Lisa?
Will I be hung in your living room, bedroom, or bathroom?
Did my painter paint me well according to your taste?
Or did you think that the oil paint he used on me was just a waste?
Can't you see I dressed up well to look pleasant
Trying hard not to look like a peasant?
I stayed still for hours to please you
Paid you the respect that you're due
You complimented me in my simple attire
While others conceived my situation as a satire
You unveiled my timidness with your persistence
You made me feel special and valued my existence
But all of a sudden you changed
I was locked up inside the closet in vain
I followed your every command
Fearful to contradict and of your severe reprimand
You always told me I looked beautiful and exotic
That's how you got me all naked and ecstatic
You told me you love me so dearly
But why put me in an auction to show my bare body?
You said I am your queen, am I not?

Asking me to reign your kingdom was just your plot
Your eyes were on my hard-earned treasure
Me sweating in blood was your kind of pleasure
Can't you see the sadness in my eyes?
The glow was slowly washed away by the tears whenever I'd cry
You used to say I have a captivating smile
How can I still have it after tasting your bile?
Please treat me like a woman from the side of your rib
Can't you see I have so much love to give?
Don't let me be stolen just for you to see
That my creator made me valuable and equal to thee.

My Blue Sky

MY BLUE SKY

Into the blue, blue sky
My thoughts are flying high
Melancholic moments wrap me in deep silence
My eyes are fixated at the clouds as they are slowly passing by
So many things floating in my mind
Clouds of memories, both gray and white
It would have been better if it's just a mere reverie
But my heart carries the clouds full of painful memories
From the breathtaking blue sky to a slow Cirrus formation
Then when reality sets in
Cumulus, Stratus, and Nimbus
All come rushing in
Into the blue, blue sky as I stare
The rain starts falling from my eyes
I ask myself, "Why am I crying?"
When all I should see is the beautiful sun that's shining
Please, Lord, help me understand
That these clouds are your favors to help bring the spring rain
You're teaching me to learn from all of my pain.

Burned Candle

BURNED CANDLE

You light up the wick of my burned candle
As I am slowly melting from the heat that I can't handle
Molded in a society where I am considered inferior
I was judged according to my exterior
You light up the wick of my burned candle
My problems are like the wind that makes my fire dwindle
Others tried to snuff out my flame
After they used me, they let me take the blame
You light up the wick of my burned candle
I almost died but you kept my fire kindled
You kept me protected so I can continue to fight
Did you let me flicker so I can share some light?
My faith is the fire and I am the burned candle
I believe that my existence is to assume a mantle
Please, Lord, don't keep me off your sight
Let my fire burn bright in this cold dark night.

Bridge

BRIDGE

On this shaky hanging bridge of life,
Between the mountains of wrong and right
Where the winds of uncertainty can push you to the edge
No matter how hard you fight
You bravely crossed the bridge, one step at a time
While reminding yourself that you'll be all right
But then strong winds knocked you off,
You started crying and screaming with so much fright
You managed to hang on to the rope of faith
While praying with all your might
You shouted, you pleaded, you looked on both sides of the bridge
But there was not a single soul in sight
You thought of letting go
But then he came along, grabbed your arm,
Pulled you up while holding on to you so tight
With a grateful heart you said,
"Thank you, Lord, for saving me
You've always been my forgiving and loving knight."

River

RIVER

Running river is speaking to me
Carrying away the mud
That stains my soul
Let it flow
Let it run
Let it cleanse this rock until the grime is gone
Running river is speaking to me
Carrying away the gravel
That's causing affliction
Let it flow
Let it run
Let it bring comfort to my prickling soles
Running river is speaking to me
Carrying away the sand
That's getting out of hand
Let it flow
Let it run
Let it be whatever has been planned
Running river is speaking to me
Bright as a crystal in Revelation
Filling my pores that are thirsty
Let it flow
Let it run
Let it proceed from the throne of God and of the lamb.

Little Brown Sparrow

LITTLE BROWN SPARROW

Chirp, chirp, chirp
Was all I could hear
Hearing you sing
Uplifted my sunken zeal
Were you singing for me?
Little brown sparrow
As you stood there with grace
On my porch's wooden beam
How soothing was your voice
As you sang your praise for him
Little brown sparrow
Were you guiding me?
Aphrodite's sacred bird
Of true love and spirituality
Your visit was short
But you made me feel loved
Little brown sparrow
You're a gift from up above
I did not understand
The lyrics of your song
But your hymn was enough
To make me sing along

You must have felt
How my heart was aching
You must have felt
How my spirit was shaking
Little brown sparrow
With brown fuzzy feathers
That keeps you warm
Even without your embrace
True love was indeed your charm.

Soft Wind

SOFT WIND

You're the soft wind
Teasing me,
Blowing my hair
In different directions
You're the soft wind
Wrapping my entire body,
It is cool and so refreshing
You're the soft wind
Touching my face
When tears are falling
You're the soft wind
That I breathe in
Keeping me alive and hoping
"Thank you, Lord," I pray
As I stand on my porch,
Feeling your presence
Through the soft wind that's blowing.

Stranger Danger

STRANGER DANGER

"Hi, how are you?"
It felt so sincere
But deep inside
I have this fear
I was confused
I thought that was nice
But I can't talk to strangers
It's not wise
I am not rude,
So I said, "Hello there!"
"I am from here, and you must be from somewhere?"
Some painful memories
I suddenly remembered
How once I trusted
A deceitful stranger
From a distance
He managed to put me in a trance
He played his music
And made me dance
I followed every beat
And swayed my hips like a fool
His music was hypnotizing
I lost my heart and lost my soul
So please forgive me

If I have to go
I know I can't judge you
From your one "hello"
Even though friendship
Is what you probably yearned
"Stranger danger"
Is what I learned.

My Shell

MY SHELL

In my shell
I just want to hibernate
Cut my heart out and refrigerate
Leave a hollow space in my chest
So from pain, I will have some rest
I just want to stay inside my shell
Where my fear and anxiety dwell
Let my scream be left silent
Hide the tears behind my smile like it's nonexistent
Let me hide inside the shell
Because trauma is worse than I can tell
Maybe time will let it heal
When I'm no more dumb and numb as steel
I'll just glance at the moon from where I hide
Let its light shine my darkest night
Let my love's memory keep me warm
Inside my shell where there's no harm.

Snowflake

SNOWFLAKE

Please don't touch me
I am a snowflake
A snowflake that easily melts
I can easily melt from the heat of your warm beautiful fingers
Or to your playful whispers
My complexity is delicate
My heart easily breaks
I was molded from a droplet
Hanging on to a dust
Freezing atmosphere made me who I am
A crystalline teardrop
Please don't touch me
Let me enjoy my short life span
I want to glow with the snow
Even just for a little while
I would love to be formed
Into a snowman that you will really like
Or be molded into a snowball
For your fun snowball fights.
But my heart is too delicate
It would never survive
Your palms are too warm
I melted again way too fast
Even without cruel intentions

This snowflake didn't last
Now I am back again to liquid
With just a simple touch
A teardrop from the sky
And into the thin air, I shall rise
Please don't touch me once I'm formed
To the wind, just let me fly, glide, and dive
You can look, but please don't touch
For I am a snowflake that easily melts
My complex structure may be beautiful
But I am too sensitive to touch.

Light Walks into My Life

LIGHT WALKS INTO MY LIFE

Glittering scarf covering her hair
One hand holding one edge
As she partly covers her seductive stare
Painted eyes and lips
To accentuate her beauty
Expensive perfume worn all over her body
In the dark alley
She's well dressed to lure
Men with lustful desire
See her as a cure
Every night, she stands there waiting
For someone to take her
Pay her by the hour with some shiny silver
"Sinful woman" is how she is called
People gather around her to stone her
Until she's dead and cold
Face filled with horror and shame
Lightened up when Jesus came
He is the light that walked into her life
Drives away seven demons
That are eating her alive
She washes his feet with her tears and expensive oil

Forgiveness for her sins is all she's asking for
From sinner to saint
Her life has never been the same
You and I, we're the modern-day Mary Magdalene
Life full of darkness because of our sins
So if repentance we truly seek
God's grace we will surely keep
His only son to us he gave
So we can all be free and be saved
Jesus is the truth
Jesus is the life
Jesus is the light that walks into my life.

My Soul

MY SOUL

Hidden inside this body
A universe on its own
Spawned from a breath
To rule over the flesh
It feeds on the intangible
Strengthened by experience
Everything in its encounter
Gives more meaning to its existence
It fights with my will
By whispering words of guilt
Trying to stop my fall
Down to eternal fires of hell
The book of wisdom
Serves as its guide
Some verses to follow
So I can walk towards the light
Faith, hope, and love
Are what it aims to show
In the midst of all the chaos
My God, this soul just wants to be with you
Hidden inside this body
A universe on its own
Traveling through endless time
Trying to find its way home.

Looking Glass

LOOKING GLASS

Looking glass
Clear as water
It speaks the truth
Of what I see whenever I look
Looking glass
What do I see?
A perception of me?
Or an image of reality?
Looking glass
Let me admire those curves and wrinkles
Beyond those facial lines and freckles
Let me look at me a little closer
Looking glass
Have I failed to see?
The real reflection of thee
Of what my Maker wants me to be.

Graceful Shore

GRACEFUL SHORE

As the sea touches the shore
It always brings back memories
Of all the love you have given me
Despite all my deficiencies
As the sea touches the shore
And washes away the sand on my feet
Your love cleanses my soul
Forgiving my sins that bury me whole
As the sea touches the shore
Your love for me I can behold
Your never-ending grace
Is the seawater that never fails to resurface.

How Can I Thank You?

HOW CAN I THANK YOU?

How can I thank you
For my everyday blessings
Like waking up to a brand-new day every morning?
How can I thank you
For your heart is so forgiving
The sins from all the temptations that I continue to keep fighting?
How can I thank you
For my needs that you're constantly providing
From the air that I am breathing to the food that I am consuming?
How can I thank you enough
For your love that is so amazing?
I know that no matter what I do
I am not deserving
"How, Oh Lord?" I pray
"How can I thank you every day?"

Counting

COUNTING

Have you ever stopped yourself
From wanting something you desire?
Have you ever tried distracting yourself from thinking
Of something that's burrowing into your mind?
Have you ever smiled while your
Heart is ripping inside?
"Will I survive this drama?"
Has this question ever crossed your mind?
Almost eight billion people on this planet
Is there someone like me with the same emotional racket?
Almost eight billion people on this planet
What chaos it will be if we're all suffering from the same anxiety
What keeps me calm when I need an emotional balm?
Lots and lots of prayers
As I look for the answers
I have been counting my blessings
To remind me that God will help me get through
Whatever challenges I am facing
He is always there continuously guiding
So as soon as I wake up, I start counting.

How I Read You

HOW I READ YOU

You're so pleasing to my eyes and so hard to ignore
You might look old, but you are well built in structure
Bulky, hard, and with appealing color
You are the kind I would certainly go for
Looking at you standing in that wooden corner
I can't help but smile and wonder
You got me thinking and made me eager
To know you more, and so I went closer
I checked out your title and your author
You got me excited to be your reader
That old book smell that certainly lingers
I still found myself liking that musty odor
With curiosity, I removed you from between the metal binders
And gently held your hardbound cover
Then I opened your first page and felt your smooth paper
I looked for a seat and turned your pages, just a browser
But you were too good to let go as I dug deeper
There was so much in you that I wanted to discover
My imagination, you made it wilder
Your stories made my heart beat faster
You made me cry but also stronger
You taught me skills and made me wiser
You became my teacher and entertainer
If only everything in your pages I can remember
You're a beacon of hope for the truth and knowledge seeker
So I thank God for books and all the writers.

I Thank God for Poetry

I THANK GOD FOR POETRY

You're like a ray of sun that lights up my day
Such beautiful words like flowers, every day you send my way
Your love is like fire that ignites my passion for poetry
So with hope in my heart, I opened a window of opportunity
But your heavy cloud rained on all our possibilities
Your love made me lose all my faculties
You brought thunder and lightning that I feared
You left me out in the cold
With my heart severed
I looked up to the heavens and prayed so hard
This pain inside is crippling that I can't disregard
"What should I do?"
"What should I do?"
"Oh Lord," I pray
A lost soul in desperation
I can't seem to find my way
Silence in my room during this period of social isolation
I found my inner strength with the help of my newfound passion
So with my pen and some papers,
I continued to write
I thank God there's poetry,
Now my heavy heart feels light.

True Happiness

TRUE HAPPINESS

When I am sick
You comfort me
When I am lonely
You are there for me
When I needed an ear
You didn't just hear
You listened to my prayers
And always showed you care
You're not just a friend
You're someone I can depend on
Even if I go astray
You help me find the right way
With your love and forgiveness
God, with you there's true happiness.

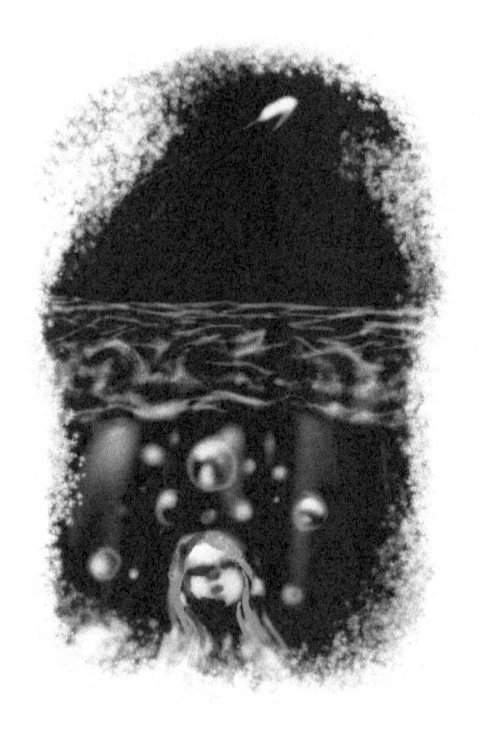

The Deafening Silence

THE DEAFENING SILENCE

The deafening silence in my room opened a gate
That brought back my childhood memories to me
When I used to live in a very crowded city
Where the noise and the pollution did not bother me
When I enjoyed life even in our state of poverty
Back then, I ate whatever food we could afford
And wore clothes even when ripped.
My brothers, sisters, and relatives,
We all had good relationships
I had a great time in school and found true friendship
My childhood was good despite our financial hardship
The deafening silence in my room also became a vortex
That sucked me into the realm of negativity
It made me think of current events and their complexity
"What am I doing?" I asked myself in perplexity
I should be enjoying this moment of silence and liberty.

Chaos

CHAOS

In the midst of chaos
I was silenced
Mouth covered with a mask
Face shielded with tasks
In the midst of chaos
I was isolated
Struggling to be distant
But longing for a bond
In the midst of chaos
Relativity is warped
Distortion of mind and heart
Led to a broken heart
In the midst of chaos
I discovered me
Someone I want to be
I am caged but free
In the midst of chaos
I have peace of mind
I found more value of time
And the true meaning of life
In the midst of chaos
God opened my eyes
He gave me strength to survive
And I am grateful to be alive.

Frontline

FRONTLINE

With impermeable gown, goggles, PAPR, and N95 mask
I salute your courage to fulfill the heavy task
You never give up, no matter how risky
Facing all the health hazards, oh so bravely
Now with PPE shortage everywhere
You're all facing a grave danger
Still you're trying to save the lives of different strangers
COVID-19 flooding the news
So everyone can be aware
It really breaks my heart knowing that others don't even care
Please help the caregivers
By simply following the rules
Keep your distance, wash your hands, and don't be a fool
Remember just like you, they also want to stay alive
It just so happens in their hearts
They feel responsible in helping you survive
To the health care professionals and all the frontliners
To the people in the military service, police departments, and firefighters
To the volunteers and everyone who is helping out there
Thank you so much for showing us
How much you really care

Hope for Humanity

HOPE FOR HUMANITY

Shades of red, blue, green, orange, and yellow
It's sundown but I am filled with hope for tomorrow
The darkest of night is here, but in my heart a rainbow appeared
Side by side, the unity of different colors calms down my fears
In the solitude of this horrific moment
Where everyone is far, yet trying to be present
Like a child watching and learning in silence
Humanity is praying for its continued existence
Have you seen the beautiful colors of the heavens as the sun goes down?
I know it will surely make you smile and get rid of that frown
On the rooftops where everyone is clapping
Making noise for the heroes who are sacrificing
Don't just look but experience the beauty of humanity
It's quite uplifting to a soul that's weary
Take a moment to rejoice, to treasure, and to enjoy
Another day on this earth that others try to destroy
Because the painful truth of reality
Is that life is quite short for some
That's why I am always grateful
For each day that comes.

My Pep Talk

MY PEP TALK

Relax and contract
Flex and stretch
How easy is that
Nope, you got to give it all you got
Sweat it all out
To get rid of some fats
Easy to say, but it's more than that
"Take it easy"
"Take your time"
"Slowly but surely"
"You'll get the result in no time"
"Be patient with yourself"
And that's what I am trying to do
I am talking to myself
As to what I am supposed to do
Sometimes we need to feel pain
In order to gain what we want to attain
Taking care of our temple
Is not just mind and soul
But also taking care of our body
Is a part of what makes us feel whole.

With My Eyelids Closed

WITH MY EYELIDS CLOSED

Keeping my eyelids closed
I am shutting down the curtains of my realm
To calm down the vortex of restless thoughts
That are rapidly sucking me in
To relieve the cramped-up
Fibers that are holding my bones
To dust off the rust that's eroding my self-preservation
And let my soul rest from all the guilt of sins
As I keep my eyelids closed
I'm immersed into meditation
Focusing on all the positive energy
The serenity that exudes in nature
I want to bathe in all its purity
And let the silence transcend over the chaos within me
Keeping my eyelids closed
I listen to the whispering wind as it passes by
I listen to the birds as they sing their lullabies
I listen to the leaves dancing in their own symphony
I listen to the crickets' intermittent stridulation
I listen to the sound of my slow respiration
And finally, I listen to my caged soul screaming for salvation
With my eyelids closed

In the beginning, all I can see is darkness
Dilemmas of my life's circumstances
Inflating the balloon that wants to explode inside my chest
As the welling tears seep through the crevices of my porous walls
I continue to meditate
Until a ray of light paves its way to give me hope
Lifting up the spirit with burdens
Enlightening my mind's catechism
Releasing the tension from my body's exhaustion
Removing life's toxicity that served as its poison
I am overwhelmed by the power of meditation.

Into the Woods

INTO THE WOODS

Footsteps yearn for an adventure
But my soul just wants to be with nature
Into the woods where the tall trees grow
I seek both needs to relieve my sorrow
Amazed by the canopy of the luscious green leaves
Tree branches as they reach out
With entwined twigs they dance
To the rhythm of the wind's masterpiece
As the sun rises and penetrates
The thickness of the forest with its golden rays
It creates a majestic art
A kaleidoscope of shadows
That gives delight to my heart
Fallen trees lying on the ground
A sculptured piece of lightning bolt
The moss spreading to its trunk
An astonishing sight by the circle of life
While I listen to the birds and other animals chatter
Taking turns and conversing with each other
They're emphasizing the harmony in understanding
If only we would really care to listen
Solace in solitude
Silence that brought me peace
Wonders of God's creation

Have rewarded me with bliss
Into the woods, I came to explore
Not just nature's wonder but to know myself more
Into the woods I discovered
Life's simple pleasure of being one with nature
Into the woods
I went to hike with my friends
And I had a good time
I enjoyed the fresh air
I enjoyed the beauty of nature
But most importantly
I enjoyed my friends' company.

Before I Go to Sleep

BEFORE I GO TO SLEEP

Before I go to sleep
Like a critic in a movie theater
In my mind, I watch my whole day's premiere
Reflections from the time I opened my eyes
Until I finally kiss the day goodbye
Have I been good to everyone?
Did I say a word that would offend anyone?
Did I do my best to care?
And to others, my blessings have I shared?
Can I sleep with conscience clear?
Can I face him someday without fear?
Did I make my father proud?
To the heavens, is my prayer loud?
Did I ask for his forgiveness?
I am not perfect and he knows all my weakness
To all his blessings, did I express my gratitude?
Through all my battles, he has given me fortitude
Before I close my eyes to sleep
I pray that my soul he will keep
I want to be with him someday
Just in case I don't live to see another day.

My Painting

BEFORE I GO TO SLEEP

Before I go to sleep
Like a critic in a movie theater
In my mind, I watch my whole day's premiere
Reflections from the time I opened my eyes
Until I finally kiss the day goodbye
Have I been good to everyone?
Did I say a word that would offend anyone?
Did I do my best to care?
And to others, my blessings have I shared?
Can I sleep with conscience clear?
Can I face him someday without fear?
Did I make my father proud?
To the heavens, is my prayer loud?
Did I ask for his forgiveness?
I am not perfect and he knows all my weakness
To all his blessings, did I express my gratitude?
Through all my battles, he has given me fortitude
Before I close my eyes to sleep
I pray that my soul he will keep
I want to be with him someday
Just in case I don't live to see another day.

My Painting

MY PAINTING

Black is the shadow
I painted my night
Despair that creeps in
I struggle to fight
And when it comes back
I try to turn on the light
Blue is the tint
I painted my sky
Tears that filled my eyes
Turn into rain
Pouring out the sorrow
When I am in pain
Red is the pigment
I painted my flowers
Stained by the strands
Of my brush that bleeds
Dripping with passion
Full of mixed emotions
White is the color
I painted my soul
To be clean and pure
For my creator to behold
But my dirty hands smeared it
And turned it into gray

Green is the shade
I painted my leaves
Springs from the branches
Of my wisdom tree
With the hope to filter pollution
For others to breathe
Yellow is the hue
I painted the sun
Smiles that are radiant
Make the day bright and fun
Hoping to spread like rays
Until the day is done
The painting of my life
Every stroke imprints
True colors of me
For life is an art
Whose elegance is its significance
It is an abstract of reality.